It doesn't matter how many times they fall, what matters is how many times they get back up.

A true story that Otto told me in one
whole night

Carlos Mateo

Introduction

Otto tells how it came about:
"On my last trip to Europe, I had some things to do, I wanted to sell my house, the furniture and also my much loved car. It was a hard parting, 40 years we lived in this place and in this house and no other owners are using my things. They live in my house, which we saved from our mouths. I did most of the house building myself. We had no holidays, I worked on building the house every free minute. Then the children came, again no free minutes.

At Christmas, we bought a little dog for the children, so we were happy. Little by little we were better off financially and bought a second-hand car on installments, even the television, in color of course, which was an expensive affair back then in the 60s, was bought on installments. It was a difficult time, but we stuck together, we only bought things cheaply, or better cheaply, and we saved money back and forth. Then the children started school, we lived in a village which had about 800 inhabitants at that time. Today, there are about 25,000 inhabitants, with banks, a supermarket, a shopping center, a cinema, a municipal swimming pool, and so on.

We were not rich, but happy, and I think that was the most important thing. Later, the children left home, they started their families and the two of us were alone.

But I wanted to tell my story, although the above is also part of my story.

On my last visit, I was alone and the evenings are very long, so one longs for a beer or a glass of wine. Well, I went to a bar and since all the seats were taken, the waiter sat me at a table with a gentleman. We got acquainted, as we had been taught as children. His name was Carlos, and we got to talking, and I brought myself to tell my whole life story. Carlos asked me at the end of our conversation if he could write it down, he told me he was a writer and my narrative excited him."

When Otto came into the world, in 1937, there was a wartime atmosphere in the country and World War 2 was coming. Well, he was still too young to know anything about it, his parents lived with him in a big Bavarian city. His father worked there as an engine designer.

Otto was, I think, about 75 years old, we immediately liked each other and Otto began to talk. What I heard was a whole life with all its ups and downs.

His fate was so interesting, I had never heard anything like it before. When I think back now, I heard a whole life that night. It was pure coincidence or was it fate that we met that night. We sat together all night, talking and talking. In my mind I asked myself, why is he telling me all this?

At first, I thought he was just telling me a fairy tale, but then I realized that something was being told here that was true and Otto needed to get it all off his chest. This night with me was supposed to help Otto talk about his problems and find a way to lead a better life, even if he only had a short time until the end. Otto was a bit excited when he started talking, he was a so-called grown man. He started, which was strange, with his childhood and told me a whole period of at least 70 years. I admire Otto's memory, he told and told.

When we both parted early in the morning, I felt a relief in Otto, he had processed all the rubbish, it was already a rubbish heap or better, a rubbish dump that Otto got off his chest.

I kept putting off writing all this down, I had other things to do, but now I will write this story down because Otto's life is worth writing about.

Here you are reading a true story, a story that life wrote.

How it all began with Otto

Little Otto was born in Cologne on the Rhine in 1937. His father worked as an engineer in a company that manufactured engines. But his father did not want to stay in Cologne, he was from Thuringia, and he was drawn to the south of Germany. He applied to various companies and got a job as an engine designer in a company in Franconia. His small family moved away from Cologne, and they started a new life in Franconia. Just to remind you, Otto made his first train journey with his mother from Cologne to Thuringia when he was 3 weeks old, that's just by the way, it was his first visit, to his grandparents.

Otto, the city kid, was about three years old and grew up in a big city. The war also came to Bavaria, air raid alerts and down to the cellars, one night there was another air raid alert and the inhabitants of the whole house ran into the air raid shelter. It was a terrible attack, even in the air-raid shelter vibrations were felt and Otto was terrified, which accompanied him almost all his life. Everyone in the cellar felt that death was quite near, and it was pure luck that no bombs hit this house.

When the all-clear came, oh horror, his flat was a pure pile of rubble.

Windows were broken, doors were off their hinges, all the furniture was badly occupied, you couldn't live in that flat anymore. His father got emergency accommodation from his company where they could live to some extent. So, his parents decided that his mother and Otto should go to his grandparents' house to be somewhat safe from the terrible attacks. After all, it was safer in the village than in the city. So, he came to the small village in Thuringia.

In the middle of the preparations for the journey came the next blow: his father was drafted into the army. So, Otto came to the small village, which had 500 inhabitants on the border with Bavaria. The war was everywhere.

At the age of 6, Otto went to the local primary school, a small village school with 2 classrooms for 1 - 4 and 5 - 8.

It was not easy for the little one, school did not cause him any problems. But there is always something that creates turmoil in a quiet life. So, it was with Otto, he was scared, when he heard an airplane he immediately threw himself into the dirt, his classmates teased him, and sometimes he was even attacked. The little boy held out, he took everything, one day there was another attack on him, he was lucky and hit the worst and strongest of all the children right on the nose, so that blood splattered and the one everyone feared snapped. Otto was respected from then on and his life became calmer. That's how it is in life sometimes. Call it what you will, I think heaven helped here.

Life in the country was less dangerous, but his nerves were badly shaken; his victory in the schoolyard helped him to become braver and freer. Otto was a good student and always brought home good grades, to his mother's delight.

One day, the war was almost over and the boys were playing in the forest as usual, there were lots of weapons lying around that the German soldiers had thrown away and the children collected them. One day, the Americans were already quite close, the children found a bazooka in the forest, one of the bigger boys said, I know how this thing works, we just need a string and have to hide in the holes dug by the soldiers, then we'll try it out. No sooner said than done, the big boy fastened the string and all the children hid in the holes they had dug. Then a hiss and a crash, trees were bent or broken off and the thing was fascinating for the children. What came next was less beautiful because at the same moment the forest was shelled. The Americans were already all around. All the children were hiding in their holes, fortunately they were not hit. But the smell coming from these foxholes was terrible.

But then everything got worse, the American soldiers searched the forest and found the children in their holes. All the children were scared to death because these soldiers were blacks, and they eat little children, as was always propagated. Now it was finally over for the children. But the soldiers laughed when they saw the children and pulled them out of the holes, cleaned them and gave them chocolate, oranges and bananas to eat. The children didn't know all that because you couldn't buy anything like that during the war. They tasted it and then ate it all.

The soldiers put the children on a tank and drove them to the small village. Otto said, "We were the first to have contact with the occupation and took the village with us. So, we came home, our parents were worried because they knew we were in the forest".

Later he went to live with his other grandparents in the mill, he was no longer afraid of the American soldiers. They all knew him already. When he came to his grandparents' yard, Otto said, "there was a jeep with soldiers, and they had an interpreter with them who wanted to clarify it for my grandfather that he had to vacate his house within 12 hours because the Americans wanted it as their headquarters.

"But they didn't know my grandmother yet, who was listening to everything in the house. She came to the front door and started talking to the soldiers in American, or better still, Texan because she had grown up with her parents in Galveston in Texas. All the soldiers stood in the yard with their mouths open and the boss of them said to my grandmother, 'Mam, you don't have to go, you're one of us,'" Otto told me.

A little later the commanding officer came and asked his grandmother if the Americans could cook and eat in the house, and she had no work, everything would be done and the whole family could then eat too."

So, a few months passed and Otto spent a lot of time with the Americans, he also learned a little English and could communicate a little.

One day, the Americans left and the Russians came. It is well known what it was like then. His other grandparents, where Otto also lived with his mother, were the first to live in the small village, and they were quartered by a Russian officer. Luckily for the grandparents, one day a Russian came, drunk, and started to get violent. At that moment the officer came and the Russian was arrested. They then punished him very harshly later, we could hear him shouting.

What happened next?

School started again, the children had been given a teacher who was a cobbler and had no idea about school. That also passed and after a while things normalized and two teachers came who then taught all the children. After 8 years of school it was over. His parents, his father had returned from war or captivity meanwhile, wanted Otto to go to secondary school and do his A-levels. Unfortunately, there was nothing for it because his parents were capitalists and higher education was only possible for workers' children.

So, Otto learned farming. At the age of 14, Otto came to stay with acquaintances on a large farm to learn. It wasn't made easy for him; despite his 14 years, he had to do the same heavy work as the other helpers. But this had helped Otto to become more independent and to see life from a different perspective.

After 10 months, that was the end of it, he had to go home, his maternal grandparents had been taken away by the Russians and no one knew whether he and his parents would also be taken away.

It wasn't on that, and he studied for another year on his grandparents' farm.

The teacher at the vocational school had told his father to enrol him in the agricultural college, it was about 20 km from the village. No sooner said than done and he was accepted. In September, life began at the boarding school of the agricultural college.

It must have been a wonderful time, Otto raved about this boarding school. He told me he learned a lot that year. He went on holiday with the school to the island of Rügen, it was a great experience for him. Furthermore, he. Formed groups with the pupils. On this holiday, the nights were longer than the days and everything was great fun.

At harvest time it was so common or compulsory that all pupils of agricultural colleges had to help with the duck. They were taken by bus to the various cooperatives, it was so common in the GDR, and they had to work hard. They slept on straw in an old glue factory, he said, "we weren't used to that, but it was a lot of fun".

The food wasn't great, but we all organized something, and so we had plenty to eat."

 "As it happens, my father got an offer from his old job in the big city in Bavaria to work in his profession again, and he couldn't refuse. So, my technical school

days came to an end after one year,"
Otto said.

But it was practically impossible to move legally to the West. A friend of his father's had found out from the constitution that it said anyone could take up residence wherever they wanted. This was the justification for applying for and getting an exit permit. It was a long and stony road, but it was successful.

Simultaneously, Otto had found a job at the tractor station in town, working in the fields with a small tractor.

In the neighboring town, right on the state border, there was often a cinema and almost all the young people from the village went the 4 km to the cinema because they lived close to the border with Bavaria. It was over at 10 in the evening, but that evening it had snowed and the boys had a great snowball fight. As it happens, the police came and because it was past curfew, they were all arrested and sent to the local jail. They were locked until 6 in the morning, when they were all free to go.

In December of the same year, his father and he were given the exit permit, and they had 24 hours to leave the country. They took a taxi to the train station and after the controls were over, they started their journey. After about 1 hour they passed the border and a new l

life began, or was to begin, his father
and he were really puffing away.

A new life begins

The new life began, they came to the
city and his father's company had
provided a company flat. Otto, he was
almost 18 years old, came to a new
environment, actually he should know it,
he had already been there as a child
because he was still small, he didn't
remember. The people spoke a different
dialect, and it sounds strange, but
communication within the German lands
was somewhat difficult. When he came

to the village then, he spoke this dialect and the communication was funny, and now it was the same again. The traffic, cars, trams and lots of people made him nervous. His father looked for connections for him so that he could settle in better, and he got into conversation with a gentleman who directed a chamber choir. So, Otto became a singer. He enjoyed that a lot. The choir was well known and had a good name. The whole choir went to a music festival in Stuttgart, where many choirs from Germany performed their songs and the chamber choir contributed with the premiere of the Carmina Burana by Carl Orff to the festival. The most prominent audience member was German President

Theodor Heuss, who shook hands with all the singers from the Chamber Choir at the end.

Singer was handsome, but he always had empty pockets. Since he was used to working, he kept looking and found an advertisement in the newspaper, wanted to recruit for the newspaper. He applied and got the job. The pay was: commission for each subscription sold and 20 marks per day. For a whole week, he went from house to house in the villages unsuccessfully. With his dialect, he was difficult to understand and people didn't order anything. What was the end of it? He was fired as a canvasser, but for that week he got 20 marks for each day. His first earned a hundred, he was proud to have so much money.

He spotted an ad in the daily paper, a petrol station was looking for a car washer. He told me, "I don't remember what they wanted to pay". Car washing was back-breaking work, all manually and then polishing. He started but nobody told him how to do it, what to wash, so he started, it only lasted 1 week, then it was over.

There was a similar agricultural college, his father said he could continue his studies there. But he was rejected, what he had learned did not fit into the program of this school. He thought his dialect didn't fit.

Otto kept looking and one day found an advertisement for an apprentice in a wholesale electrical shop. He went and applied, working 6 days a week. They paid 40 marks a month for the first year, but it didn't matter, he then had a steady job and could continue studying if he wanted. This was a small company, a married couple with a son and 2 daughters. They sold mixers at fairs all over Germany and the first thing Otto had to do was get his driving license 3 because none of the family had a driving license anymore, it was taken away from them because they drove drunk. He didn't think badly, I got my driving license for free. Otto was on the road all over Germany, setting up trade fair stands, delivering and then back to the office. It went well for a year, then they went bankrupt and Otto was back on the street. Meanwhile, his language had improved and a friend told him that they were looking for apprentices in a real electrical wholesaler. He did nothing but go and started there straight away. Since he had already finished the first year, he started the second. His wage was already princely, 100 marks a month. He studied for two more years and then took his final exams. On the side, he had a job in a travel agency as a tour guide. Every weekend in summer he went by bus to Austria and in winter to South Tyrol. He got paid for each trip and the passengers also gave him a tip, which he shared with the chauffeur.

After his apprenticeship, Otto worked in various companies in the city and then went to the capital to work as a salesman for an electrical wholesaler. Here he earned good money, attended the evening university of the DAG and studied business administration there. Well, as life goes, Otto met a girl, fell in love, and they got married. It was a good marriage, they had 2 boys and Otto got a good job in Italy as an export clerk, he was paid decently. His family lived in Germany, he had bought a house, and so he always went to Italy on Monday morning at 3 o'clock and came back on Saturday.

He and his family were doing well, and they were happy, he was satisfied with his work and the company also appreciated him. So, as a Christmas present for himself and a wife, he got a flight ticket to New York, a hotel voucher for 10 days and the necessary pocket money. Time passed quickly and after a few years he started his own business in Germany. He sold the company's products and took on other companies. Things were going well and Otto thought, now you're set for life. Everything was right, his little family was developing splendidly, his wife was helping in the company, what more did he want.

But I think he was doing too well, there came a time in Italy when almost all the companies went on strike and the economy came to a virtual standstill, delivery problems, poor quality, paid goods were not delivered, so it was a total mess. But the crowning glory of it all was that one of his best customers in Germany sold his company to a housing association, they had taken over everything and ordered Otto to their office on 23 December. As there were still outstanding invoices, Otto thought he would get the money and finish the year well. The management said they would only pay 50% of the outstanding bills, if he didn't agree to that, they would declare bankruptcy for this purchased company, then he would get nothing. A nice Christmas present. Otto ended up having to file for bankruptcy because 2 other big customers got into trouble. He could no longer pay his debts. He also had to deal with crises. Otto no longer had any income, and he did not want to touch his savings, especially as he would lose everything through the bankruptcy, but the savings were invested elsewhere and were safe for him.

To live, he took on various jobs that were not of long duration but brought in money. So one day he met a gentleman who imported food, especially meat. He made Otto a good offer and his wife then also worked in this company.

Since Otto had the opportunity to find out about this company through his business studies, and when he was alone in the office one day, he made a list of the life span of this company. The result was that this company would not grow old. They were looking for new meat suppliers abroad and Otto was given the assignment to look for new suppliers of beef in South America, why shouldn't he take this trip, which was paid for, even though he knew the company was not going to get old.

Otto was in Paraguay for 2 weeks, got to know the country and its people and travelled almost the whole country. He was travelling with a German who was setting up the telephone network for

Telecom, and so he got to see a lot. The country inspired him and when he came back, he told his wife, I want to go to this country. Meanwhile, the company he worked for was almost ready to go bankrupt, and it didn't take two weeks before it filed for bankruptcy. Otto stayed in the office with his wife to wind up this company. The bailiff was the daily customer and Otto could help wind up justly.

An old friend of his, he was a sergeant in the German army, founded a holiday camp for normal and thalidomide children in the Bavarian mountains. The children lived in the mountains for a few weeks, it was like an Indian camp, there were horses for the disabled children, and much more. Otto had nothing to do and so his friend asked him if he would like to help out for a while. He agreed and he and his wife started helping at the camp. They liked it and meanwhile they prepared everything for emigration from Germany. (For 8 weeks they helped to make the children have a good time, then the day came to say goodbye and many of the children had tears in their eyes). It was not easy for Otto and his wife to part with their beloved children.

Now they went by car to Gran Canaria, rented a bungalow and lived there for almost 2 years. The children went to the American school and learned English as well as Spanish. As fate would have it,

Otto was at the airport and bought a German newspaper, it fell on the floor and the advertisement page opened. There were many offers from Paraguay. Otto wanted to go there to see if there was anything for him. So, he flew to South America.

I call it coincidence, the newspaper, the page that came up first with the offers, then on the plane a gentleman sat next to him and as is so usual they got into conversation. He was a dentist in Frankfurt am Main and had land and cattle in Paraguay. Since Otto had no idea about this country, he had a good contact person in his seat neighbor. They then also stayed in the same hotel, and he introduced him to his friend, a

German-Argentinean who had a wine factory. He was then invited to dinner by this gentleman, and they chatted. The South American friend of Hans the dentist, was called Julio and during the conversation he said that he had some land that he wanted to sell. He said it was 50,000 hectares, and he wanted to found a colony and sell it to German and also German-Brazilians. Hans asked Otto if he wasn't interested in buying a plot of land or marketing the project with Julio.

Otto is always a bit hasty, and so he said, o.k., we'll sell it. But he had never done anything like this before, and later he thought, if only this goes well.

So, he flew back to Gran Canaria and sorted out his things there, told his wife and said, "I want to earn some money there and prepare everything so that you can come and take the children with you". So, a new adventure began and Otto flew back to Paraguay.

Coincidences played a big part in Otto's life and here is another such coincidence. There was a German Jesuit priest who lived and worked in southern Brazil, and he wrote a letter asking if he had any land for his parishioners to sell because families in Brazil were big and people's lands were getting smaller and smaller because every child got a plot of land when they married.

So, he answered the letter of Father Gruber (a Jesuit priest to whom Pope Pius had issued a letter with permission to work and preach anywhere in the world) Father Gruber was an outstanding man with a difficult and painful life (he was imprisoned in a penal camp in Yugoslavia after the war, but did not want to be released until the last prisoner was released, you can find his summary of experience on the internet - Wendelin Gruber).

So one day a message came from Father Gruber that a delegation from his parish was coming to see the country. And they came, they came in a VW bus, over 20 people crammed in like herrings, and made the long journey of over 4000 km from Rio Grande do Sul to Paraguay. They were thrilled and he wrote the first contracts. The plots were all 20 hectares, people could buy as many plots as they wanted. After this visit, more and more German-Brazilians came to buy plots, many stayed right away and started to build a house and cultivate the land. Then German buyers also came and settled there. Today it is a well-functioning colony, with a school, a church, a small hospital and of course a church. Father Gruber died in Rome in 2002.

Paraguay, which became his second home

So, Otto came to Paraguay, his family still living in Gran Canaria. As with all business with him, it started to do well, Paraguay was very much in demand in Germany at that time, and it is again today. He also bought 400 hectares of land, situated on a stream, and built himself a little house where he could live and sleep on his land.

He rented a house in Asunción, the capital, and could have his family join him. The children went to the American school and a good life began for them. The circle of friends grew and there were many invitations. Otto was appreciated in this country. They lived in this house in Asunción for 3 years and felt comfortable.

One day, a new client came from Germany and Otto showed him the land, then they went to his farm, meanwhile he had also bought 30 young cattle with a bull and the client asked him what he wanted for the farm. The offer this customer made him was such that Otto just couldn't say no and sold his farm of 400 hectares.

This proves again, somehow everything works out the way you didn't think it would, but this price of the offer was flawless. Otto moved to the Brazilian border to a farm of 2000 hectares, which

he had sold to a German, as a manager.
It was a beautiful farmhouse there and
Otto lived in it for 2 years.

One day an acquaintance, who had a
trade in agricultural articles, told him that
a Japanese man wanted to sell his farm
of 60 hectares, Otto and his wife looked
at it and bought it.

The farm grew soy, wheat and maize as
well as vegetables and tomatoes. All 4
of them moved to this farm and planted
tomatoes and vegetables. Every day in
the morning, the fruits were harvested
and then immediately driven to the next
town and sold.

It was a good time, he knew the work, he had learned it once. Otto planted the rest of the land with soy beans in the summer and maize and wheat in the winter.

Otto also owned a small plot with bananas and mandarins, there were many tree fruits on this small farm and 3 ponds for which Otto bought fish. This small farm had everything you can think of, chickens for eggs, rabbits for slaughter, ducks and also 2 geese. Otto baked his bread, it was of high quality. And so, they lived almost independently as self-supporters.

His two boys had many friends in town and for the weekend they were always away and came back on Sunday evening. The closest neighbors from Otto's farm were 1 Japanese, 1 Brazilian 2 Paraguayans and some more, they exchanged, one had potatoes, Otto had tomatoes, the other had meat, one had milk and so on. So, life was completely independent in the food sector. Otto and his wife often went into town to visit good friends. So, it gave life a good sense.

If there was a problem, Otto quickly found the solution. He had water from a spring that gave water for 3 ponds. Here Otto tapped to pump drinking water into an elevated tank to supply his house and 2 others. He had electricity through a windmill that stored electricity in batteries, so he had light and could watch local television.

Otto now had electricity and running water, he has taken a shower and most importantly, a flush toilet, it was the only one in a 10 km radius.

He told me that he kept looking for danger and when an offer came from the government for him to go out with a pilot to plant marijuana in the vast forests, he agreed. For two years he flew with this pilot once a week for 3 hours over the forests and photographed the plantations. The government then used crop dusters to destroy them.

One day at night Otto heard a voice in his sleep saying to him "Get out as soon as possible, there is great danger", he woke his wife and told her. She said, order a truck from our friend tomorrow morning, and we'll start packing right now and get everything ready that we want to take with us. That's what happened. Otto informed his friend and phoned a friend in the capital, he told him everything, and he asked him if there was a house to rent. The friend wanted to look around. When they started at noon, he received a message with the address of his new flat. The truck started immediately, he had the new address and Otto with his wife and children then followed by car. They arrived the other morning, the truck was already there, and they unloaded everything and set up home. It was a nice house with a swimming pool, and it was nice to live there.

About 1 week later Otto got the news that the pilot he was travelling within the plane had been shot. His wife told him the voice saved our lives. So, Otto started a new life after his 10 years on the farm.

Otto's time in the house got too long, and he said he wanted to look for a job, so he came home in the evening and said I have rented a well-known

Pariliada, we will open next week and start grilling meat. As usual with Otto, this business went extremely well, they had many guests and the income was also excellent. After two years, it was 2 February 1990, tanks were driving on the street in the evening, he thought it was a military exercise, and they had guests from the government, who suddenly paid quickly and disappeared and then many journalists came, they all wanted to make phone calls. It was the day of the revolution in which the government was overthrown. We were open all night because new guests kept coming. When it became day, the whole spook was over. There was a new president and a new government. We opened again, but things were not the same.

Otto had inherited the mill as a child and so the obvious thing was, we go back, so Otto flew to Germany to stake his claim to his inheritance because meanwhile his relatives were not idle and had all filed theirs claim, everyone had inherited. There was a will, which was in front of the clerk, and so Otto could take over his property.

What had happened in Paraguay simultaneously?
Slowly all the business was getting back on track, but what it used to be, it wasn't anymore. In addition, there was theft and robbery, so Otto decided to cancel

the lease because he didn't want to
work only for the costs. What to do now,
no more business and starting a new
one was far too much of a risk.

He flew back to Paraguay, sorted
everything out there and then went back
to Germany for good, his wife came one
month later, the children were married
meanwhile and stayed in the country.

Germany, a new beginning

He worked with a laborer to renovate
the old mill, which was not in good
condition. They made it habitable as
best they could, they finished the work
in a month, and his wife joined them.

Otto was no longer an emigrant or a native, and in the small village where he grew up he was a stranger.

Together with his wife, he opened a small supermarket, which was also well-used by the inhabitants, but then a large shopping center came 20 km away, and the small supermarket was only visited for goods that had run out or were needed quickly. What was the conclusion: he had to close his shop.

His wife fell ill during this time and the doctors diagnosed bowel cancer. She was operated on and then sent to rehab, came back home but after 3 months he had to call the paramedics again, and she was taken back to hospital, then rehab and from there straight back to hospital. It was a terrible year for Otto. Every day he drove a few 100 km to the hospital to visit his wife, but she never recovered and he had to bury her in August.

Otto was destroyed, he didn't have much desire to live anymore either, but as it was, he heard that voice again that had saved his life once before, it said something like: "why are you getting upset, why are you worrying, you have many problems at the moment. Why don't you send all your problems to the universe, let it help you"?

The next morning he stood, raised his head and said, "dear God, I hereby hand over all my worries and problems to you, you do what you want with them, but leave me alone with them".
Otto said he felt much better after that.

Otto had a childhood friend, he was the only one. He said to him one day, Otto, I've started a business, it's going great, and I'm earning well, I want to expand, but I don't have the money for this, can't you help me. He showed him business papers and they were promising.

Since it was a large sum, Otto went to his bank and applied for a loan in the amount his friend wanted. As security, he gave his house and his fields and he could help his friend. It couldn't go wrong, his friend had given him a look at his books, and they were excellent and Otto thought to himself, with this investment I will be well provided for in my old age. He was satisfied, he had helped his friend and from now on, he would earn a nice amount of money.

One day, Otto received a letter from the bank, the friend had filed for bankruptcy and the bank now wanted Otto to pay back the money. The friend did not think it's necessary to tell Otto his friend. That's how much a friendship is worth! Without payment, they will auction off the collateral said the bank.

Otto thought, doesn't this ever end, every time I start something new it goes well for a long time and I earn good money, but then somehow it always ends, and I lose everything again, what is that?

Auctioning, Otto said to himself, is useless, and I'm stuck with the remaining debts, it's better to sell everything, pay off the debts and maybe there will be something left over to start a new life. After he had fought a small war with the bank, the bank (the GDR wasn't quite out of people yet) wouldn't let Otto sell, they wanted to auction off. Perhaps a bank employee was also interested.

After that was settled, Otto sold his entire inheritance, paid off his bank debts and was left with 50,000 marks. With that, he wanted to start a new life again. Otto was 65 years old by then and received a small pension. He told me he couldn't live anywhere with that money, but the 50,000 would help him. Then the pension insurance company told him that he would get a widow's pension for his deceased wife. So, he said, with this money I can start over again in the Dominican Republic, we were on holiday there many years ago,

and we liked it, so I think I can live there
too.

Otto arrived well and now lives in the
Dominican Republic, he found a cheap
house, and he bought it, or rented it for
life, which is common in these countries.
He has also found a partner again and
is no longer alone.

Epilogue

In the year the Covid-19, this problem
Otto had has become even worse. Many
have lost their jobs, business owners
who had good businesses have to file
for bankruptcy, they lose their dearest
partners, many have died of the virus,

then comes the moment, what am I going to do now, they are lonely and for some the comforter alcohol helps, even drugs are common nowadays, to pay for it, they cheat and steal. Others sit gloomily at home, have no other occupation than watching television and drinking a bottle of beer.

Some had or have bought a dog to help them overcome their loneliness, it then becomes their constant companion and best friend. It becomes difficult for these people, they no longer have any drive, no desire and life is a big problem for them.

If you analyze Otto's life, the positive almost balances out with the negative.

Otto is a stand-up guy, he often fell, but
he always got up again, respect.

   Everything he started brought him
good money for a while, but then the
other side came, and he lost everything,
or at least a large part of it.
Maybe the universe is against him, but
that can't be the case, he has a big part
of good positive thoughts and through
that he always got good beginnings with
good income but somehow in his
thought process the negative came and
the universe delivered that too, usually a
little more. They can, if their thoughts
are positive, also get everything
positive. "Think positive and the
universe will reward you" is the saying.

It is well known, today it is not easy to think only positively when you see how everything is breaking down, how many are losing their livelihood.

But Otto was always lucky in his life, every time he fell on his face, he got up and had another idea to decide his life for himself.

Something always came up for Otto, an excellent job in Italy, then strikes and an economic disaster, he was not to blame in most cases, then the bankruptcy of his company, first brilliant business, then the brutal side, only paying 50% and at the same time 2 other big customers went bankrupt.

But he found a decently paid job again with the meat people and got to know his future country through that. It all looks like coincidence, the newspaper with the advertisements, the person sitting next to him on the plane, the German from Telecom who showed him a lot of the country, then Hans and Julio who made it possible for him to start a new job and earn money.

The nightly vote on the farm that saved his life, the restaurant that was doing well, then the revolution. In Germany, the supermarket, then the big shopping center. Then the biggest blow, the death of his wife, but then at night again that voice that advised him to give everything to the universe.

Then the hammer, his best friend double-crossed him, he lost his whole inheritance, but some luck, the 50,000 that was left. Now and then there is a ray of hope.

Then one day Otto flew to the Dominican Republic, he had chosen an address on the Samana peninsula on the Internet, and he is still there today. If any of you have a problem like that, do what Otto did.
It doesn't matter how many times they fall, what matters is how many times they get back up.

A true story that Otto told me in one
whole night
Carlos Mateo

Carlos Mateo Author

Born in Cologne, grew up in Thuringia
and later moved to Nuremberg. Studied
agriculture and wholesale.
Due to the death of my wife, who died of
cancer, I wrote a book about the
different ways of treating cancer. During
her illness I searched for alternative

healing methods and attended many congresses, self-published with the most famous German and international specialists. Now in my old age I have started writing again, my first paperbacks are "Your wishes and dreams come true" and "Tomorrow's Happiness starts today" and several others.

Imprint

Name: Carlos Mateo

Address: C/Mesaola2

ES 38530 Candelaria / Tenerife

E-mail: manotkur@gmail.com

Tel: +34680633108

ISBN: 9798736786190

meaning of trademark and brand
protection legislation and may therefore
be used by anyone. Despite careful
editing, errors may creep in. The author
and publisher are therefore grateful for
any comments in this regard. All liability
is excluded, all rights reserved.

Notes